Also by Marge Piercy

Fiction

GOING DOWN FAST
DANCE THE EAGLE TO SLEEP
SMALL CHANGES
WOMAN ON THE EDGE OF TIME
THE HIGH COST OF LIVING
VIDA
BRAIDED LIVES

Poetry

BREAKING CAMP
HARD LOVING
4-TELLING (*with Bob Hershon, Emmett Jarrett,*
  and Dick Lourie)
TO BE OF USE
LIVING IN THE OPEN
THE TWELVE-SPOKED WHEEL FLASHING
THE MOON IS ALWAYS FEMALE
CIRCLES ON THE WATER

Play

THE LAST WHITE CLASS (*with Ira Wood*)

Essay

PARTI-COLORED BLOCKS FOR A QUILT

Stone, paper, knife

STONE, PAPER, KNIFE

by Marge Piercy

ALFRED A. KNOPF   New York   1983

017706 ✓

/2·95

THIS IS A BORZOI BOOK
PUBLISHED BY ALFRED A. KNOPF, INC.

Grateful acknowledgment is made to the following periodicals where
most of these poems previously appeared:

*Affinities, Akros, Another Chicago Magazine, Aspect, Barnwood,
Buckle, Cedar Rock, Connecticut Poetry Review, Croton Review,
Dragonsmoke, The Guardian, Iowa Review, Kalliope, Manhattan
Poetry Review, Mid-South Writer, Mosaic, Mudfish, National Forum,
Negative Capabilities, Open Places, Partisan Review, Ploughshares,
Poetry Miscellany, Poetry Now, Poets On, Pomegranate Press, Pulp,
Sun and Moon, Tarasque, Tendril, 13th Moon, Vanderbilt Poetry
Review.*

Library of Congress Cataloging in Publication Data
Piercy, Marge.   Stone, paper, knife.   I. Title.
PS3566.I4S76   1983   811'.54   82-48050
ISBN 0-394-52802-6   ISBN 0-394-71219-6 (pbk.)

Manufactured in the United States of America
FIRST EDITION

RECEIVED ⋯⋯ 9 1983

For my mother
Bert Bernice Bunnin Piercy
who died as I was sending off this manuscript

Contents

IN THE MARSHES
OF THE BLOOD RIVER 43

MRS. FRANKENSTEIN'S DIARY

Mrs. Frankenstein

An old howitzer, a sewing machine,
a Concorde engine, chrome bumpers,
a scientist trained never to feel,
a fucking machine, a stone face
without ears to hear others,
a stomach that could digest
the most perfect beef Wellington
without letting go a belch
or ever complimenting the cook,
feet that could march over
breasts without noticing;
she found him a desperate
graduate student fucking his fist
and growing pimples like golf balls.

He whimpered of how daddy
didn't care and mommy
didn't love and nobody
rubbed his back or kissed his belly.
She upholstered him in plush,
gilded his balls and fed vitamins,
fresh fruit and sixty-eight
food supplements until he could
run up Mount Washington and back
before supper.

A is for anguish
she said, the way I feel

when you stand on my face. B
is for beautiful, like this rose.
No, you don't wipe your ass
with it usually. C is for
a very nice part of my body
with which you enjoy
a pretty part of your body;
D is for dogs and cats which
are by unimaginative people called
dumb but who speak with their bodies
wholly in articulate delight
into your hand and eye.
E is for empathy
the foundation of ethics and F
is for food which is cooked
not by a stove but by a person
and G is for garbage which
does not vanish but has to be
dealt with handily by all living
and to come, and on to Z which stood,
she learned, not for zoosphere
but, Zanzibar where he flew
to rough it escaping bourgeois
home with only a backpack,
credit cards and his rich
and pliant mistress. I am

a feeling man, he said as he returned to start divorce
proceedings.
            I have learned
to cry on demand. What I feel
is that you forgot, you bitch,
to teach me how much fun
giving pain is. But power
is the greatest kick of all,
he said, applying it to her belly.
Machines only kill, he said,
but murder becomes a man.
I act and then I weep and then
I discuss myself with therapist
and mistress. I eat money
and excrete manhood.
I am the measure of the human
and find you wanting; you
want too much.

Dry July

I think I have forgotten what rain
sounds like. Yet at dawn waking muffled
in fog and sweat I hallucinate it
pittering on the dusty leaves.
By ten the fog burns off exposing
the flat grainy sky boring
as a yawn, over us like armor.
The trees turn dull, leaves limp
as cooked spinach. Our blood
thickening, all of us bake slowly,
panting dogs, dusty blackbirds, dying
toads and quarreling lovers. On the grill
of the sand basted only by our tears
we turn spitted below the crackling sun.

You don't understand me,

you gulp, a frog suddenly on my dinner
plate hopping through the buttered noodles
blinking cold eyes of reproach.

I can interpret the language of your hands
warm under calluses. Your body speaks into mine.
We are native users of the same jangling American.

A casual remark lets ants loose in your ears.
The wrong tone drips ice water on your nape.
Waiting I finger the bruise-colored why.

Look, I can't study you like the engine
of an old car coughing into silence on wet mornings.
Can't read the convolutions of your brain through the skull.

You want hieroglyphs at the corners of your squint decoded
in perfect silence that folds into your ribbed side,
a woman of soft accordion-pleated wool with healer's hands.

I don't understand you : you are not a book,
an argument, a theory. Speak to me.
I listen, and I speak back.

The deck that pouts

My deck is furious.
I took it on six jets,
through hotels, motels
up to timberline
on a snoozing volcano
twitching like a dreaming cat.
I was seeking money
and fleeing trouble
like a storm I could outrun.
Now my cards sing disaster,
bristling swords like a porcupine.
I know it is my own psyche
I fan on the table.
Now I must stand, face upward
in a rain of blood. I must grasp
my decisions like swords.
I must bear them on my back
like wands. I must open
my five senses like doors

to the wind, I must drink down
this salty cup. I am back
in the wreck of my life,
a house a tornado flattened.
I must sleep in the rubble,
my deck under a makeshift pillow.
When we run away, what
we come back to has run
along, and now there is light
where there was shadow
and the colors have shifted brightness.
I rise to rebuild my house
of cards, of paper, here
at the meeting place of winds.

The matrimonial bed

That first winter in the middle
of the night you could not sleep
and woke me because the caress
of my unconscious breath across
your outflung knuckle roused you.
I opened my eyes to your cheek
cradled on my thigh.
                    You bear
the same name and wear
the same face, man who pretends
deep breathing gusty sleep
beside me as vainly I rub
my breasts against your back
curved away like the shell of a turtle.

A tangential death

All through the turning year of '66
(when I don't remember a spring or fall
in Brooklyn, the only seasons being
too hot and too cold, the season
of street hassling and the season of scurry-
ing through deserted streets, but always
I remember smoke on the wind
from a fire that burned in Asia)
I carried your image about with me,
a pocket Adonis, a radiant boy god
I hung garlands of novellas on,
composed in the IRT, the Haitian laundromat.

I have never felt as old as I did
then. The youngsters were in bloom.
Somewhere at a party only they were
invited to they danced all night with long
hair shimmering. I fell into lust
with maned prophetic faces in the street
and trudged home with my groceries
and rejection slips. At a party
I walked in on my husband making love
to a Columbia student. He wanted
an open relationship, he announced,
but nothing seemed open to me.

I wanted to be visible again, real
as before I married. Labels were
plastered over me till I couldn't

see out my own windows. I stuffed
envelopes for the Fort Hood Three,
marched dressed respectable but warm
and fingered you like a medal. Your songs
sounded like hope to me.
                    Then Susan
and I began dancing together, hemmed
our dresses thigh high and suddenly
she was in love and left her husband
for an activist painter, and I was in love
and didn't leave. My life lit up
from the inside like a big house
where everybody's home. My day was full
of duets, trios, quartets, choruses
and fine ruminative solos like a good
opera. I danced all night to your music
and didn't remember my quaint old lust.
I edited that season of domestic misery
out of my life. When you married Yoko,
your choice pleased me.
                    Fame
is irrational minor godhead conferred:
to be suddenly numinous, luminous
yet to eat soft boiled eggs for breakfast
and worry about stomach gas and the cat's

cough. People imagine if they ate
your brain or cock or your old clothes
they would wake up loving themselves.
People make faces before you like a fun-
house mirror, and rage, demanding
a laying on of hands to make them real.

Styles then bubbled from the bottom up.
It seemed we would simply run around
the far end of the petrified WASP grandeur
and dungeons and head for the United
Federation of Planets on the starship
Enterprise. At the SDS Regional
at Princeton I had a vision of the place
as built of stones of ossified
ruling class shit that could simply
dissolve in the acid rain. The rough
heady steam of working class energy
in good times, when everything was cheap.
The force of sex, laughter and anger
propelled our loving armies through minor
barricades.
　　　　　How do you thank someone
who gave you pleasure and was killed?
An idiot waste. You made music

neither empty nor sadistic that I swam
in like a wide warm river with a strong
but survivable current, a river that flowed
where I longed to go. You wanted
a better life for the people we both
came from, and the times are hardening fast.

A story wet as tears

Remember the princess who kissed the frog
so he became a prince? At first they danced
all weekend, toasted each other in the morning
with coffee, with champagne at night
and always with kisses. Perhaps it was
in bed after the first year had ground
around she noticed he had become cold
with her. She had to sleep
with heating pad and down comforter.
His manner grew increasingly chilly
and damp when she entered a room.
He spent his time in water sports,
hydroponics, working on his insect
collection.
         Then in the third year
when she said to him one day, my dearest,
are you taking your vitamins daily,
you look quite green, he leaped
away from her.
         Finally on their
fifth anniversary she confronted him.
"My precious, don't you love me any
more?" He replied, "Rivet. Rivet."
Though courtship turns frogs into princes,
marriage turns them quietly back.

Ragged ending

1.

The dark side of the moon,
no atmosphere between us.
Looks freeze, shattering
to shards that pierce the skin.
I am exposed here in a décolleté
black nightgown with see-through
lace in appropriate places
and an embroidered red rose.
He wears a regulation space
suit, head in a see-through
bubble. His voice issues
amplified instructions. "I view
your tears as an act
of aggression. My missiles
are trained on your secret
bases armed with warheads
that could destroy me."

2.

Love dies like a poisoned
cat vomiting.
Sleep has left my bed
as he has. They curl up
together downstairs while I
pore over scenes as if
reading the palm of a murderer.

3.

In pain all women are grey.
We endure one long hollow
endless night drilling
the marrow of our brains.
At the meeting I recognized
the right-wing woman
was voting with the feminists
because her husband is leaving.

Every middle-aged woman abandoned
by her longest love blows
in the night wind like torn
newspapers, shredding.
At two a.m. I become Sylvia
Plath; at three a.m. I turn
into Anne Sexton; at four
a.m. I turn into my mother.

4.

What do I do at midnight
with his words flittering in
my skull like bats that can't
escape a locked room? I read,
forgetting pages as I turn
them. I practice relaxation

exercises like worry beads.
I talk aloud to my cats
who wash me with rough
maternal tongues. I try
to call up the faces of those
who do love me. Silently
I scream my head off.

5.

Pain is the groundswell bass.
Pain is the drone beneath
the recitativo of conversation.
Pain lies under my feet like broken rocks.
Tears wait in my eyes,
little accidents ready to happen.

6.

There looms the person
with whom I have shared
the last seventeen years
that will never be eighteen.
I sing the old sour song
of why me? why us? how

can you shut off like a furnace
run out of fuel? I rise
every morning like a waning
moon on a new world I
do not care for but mean
to survive whole to change.

What's that smell in the kitchen?

All over America women are burning dinners.
It's lambchops in Peoria; it's haddock
in Providence; it's steak in Chicago;
tofu delight in Big Sur; red
rice and beans in Dallas.
All over America women are burning
food they're supposed to bring with calico
smile on platters glittering like wax.
Anger sputters in her brainpan, confined
but spewing out missiles of hot fat.
Carbonized despair presses like a clinker
from a barbecue against the back of her eyes.
If she wants to grill anything, it's
her husband spitted over a slow fire.
If she wants to serve him anything
it's a dead rat with a bomb in its belly
ticking like the heart of an insomniac.
Her life is cooked and digested,
nothing but leftovers in Tupperware.
Look, she says, once I was roast duck
on your platter with parsley but now I am Spam.
Burning dinner is not incompetence but war.

The man who is leaving

The man who is leaving wants nothing
but ashes in his wake. If you cry
he looks away to state, *Your pain*

*is easy for you are a figment
of my engorged imagination. Only
my pain which is actually anger is real.*

He would pull the air from your lungs,
he would draw the water from your flesh,
he would drain the blood from your veins.

He has secrets. They
swarm in him like hornets
lighting his eyes yellow.

He has plans. They put
a spring in his step
as he strides over scattered limbs.

But the sound of your voice behind
entreating for justice, reminding him
of old love sticks in his ears,

clings to his feet like mud,
something he must wash off
before it can slow his progress.

A debate on posture

When the door cracks from bottom to top,
when the sky begins to roar,
to rain copperheads and bear traps,
I can crawl under the bed, I can
if I still fit, if I pull out the old
suitcase with the winter clothes
first. The cats and I shiver there
waiting for the ceiling to fall.

My impulse is to grab an umbrella,
a garbage can lid, and charge out into it.

What I have finally learned is that
it doesn't matter much if I went
to them or they came to me, my troubles,
hip deep in copperheads and bear traps.

December 31, 1979

For ten years we have been hurtling inward,
a spaceship bound for the bottom of the colon,
the depth of the medulla oblongata.
A decade outward, a decade inward.

Does it balance? When I envision all
the Ouija boards being fingered in rooms
full of houseplants in macrame harnesses
from Bangor to San Diego I giggle

but wanly and think maybe I should breed
daylilies or study Hungarian. My friends
are all telling me what they did in previous
reincarnations as priests and dogs.

I keep wondering if we can still
manage something better in this one.

The weight

1.

I lived in the winter drought of his anger,
cold and dry and bright. I could not breathe.
My sinuses bled. Whatever innocent object
I touched, door knob or light switch,
sparks leapt to my hand in shock.
Simply crossing a room generated static.
Any contact could give sudden sharp pain.

2.

All too long I have been carrying a weight
balanced on my head as I climb the stairs
up from the subway in rush hour jostle,
up from the garden wading in mud.
It is a large iron pot supposed to hold
something. Only now when I have finally
been forced to put it down, do I find
it empty except for a gritty stain
on the bottom. You have told me
this exercise was good for my posture.
Why then did my back always ache?

3.

All too often I have wakened at night
with that weight crouched on my chest,

an attack dog pinning me down. I would
open my eyes and see its eyes glowing
like the grates of twin coal furnaces
in red and hot menacing regard.
A low growl sang in its chest, vibrating
into my chest and belly its warning.

4.

If it rained for three weeks in August,
you knew I had caused it by weeping.
If your paper was not accepted, I had
corrupted the judges or led you astray
into beaches, dinner parties and cleaning
the house when you could have been working
an eighteen-hour day. If a woman would not
return the importunate pressure of your hand
on her shoulder, it was because I was watching.
Or because you believed she thought I
was watching. My watching and my looking away
equally displeased.
                    Whatever I gave you
was wrong. It did not cost enough;
it cost too much. It was too fancy for
that week you were a revolutionary
trekking on dry bread salted with sweat
and rhetoric. It was too plain; that week
you were the superb connoisseur whose palate

could be struck like a tuning fork only
by the perfect, to sing its true note.

5.

Wife was a box you kept pushing me down
into like a trunk crammed to overflowing
with off-season clothes, whose lid
you must push on to shut. You sat
on my head. You sat on my belly.
I kept leaking out like laughing
gas and you held your nose
lest I infect you with outrageous joy.

Gradually you lowered all the tents
of our pleasures and stowed them away.
We could not walk together in dunes or
marsh. No talk or travel. You would only fuck
in one position on alternate Thursdays
if the moon was in the right ascendancy.
Oh, Cancer, Cancer, you scuttle and snap.
Go and do with others all the things
you told me we could not afford.

Your anger was a climate I inhabited
like a desert in dry frigid weather
of high thin air and ivory sun,
sand dunes the wind lifted into stinging
clouds that blinded and choked me
where the only ice was in the blood.

From something, nothing

No matter how warm are the soft
buffy feathers of your breast,
no matter with what clear cloudless
patience you wait unmuttering,
no matter what candle of hope
you burn aloft between your eyes
secure from the draft of doubt,
poor beguiled hen, that stone
will never hatch into a chick
or even a beetle.

Being left

Some letting go is like a leaf
falling from a tree; some
is water running downhill
so slowly you can hardly
see which direction the stream
snakes; some is water
leaping off a mountain to hang
in air as mist and smash
on the rocks. Some leaving
is like murder: the need
to kill the love who is
no longer loved; the need
for blood spurting
to sign finale. Why?

You walk on where you want;
you march, you fly, you
paddle. Why the urge
to raze the ground behind?
Do you believe if you left
me alive you would
be tempted to come back?
We both know
back isn't there. The tree
puts out new leaves or dies.
What you have abandoned
is not behind but far ahead
where we shall never
now arrive.

Where nothing grows

Off into the desert you march
feeling the hot wind of your anger
blow through the bones of promises.
You know no other enemy but me
who loved too long.

Whether I like it or not
I am free to hike off although
I do not choose stones and arid
spikes of cactus. I know
the desert blooms in spring
rain, and that occasional miracle
can addict. Didn't it capture me?

I follow the line of the water
course, I follow the birds
to the willow fringe, the scent
of foliage breathing, the hum
of insects in the grass.
Like water I seek my own level
and like any social beast I look
for my kind in the twilight.

But you, you have gone to the rocks
cursing the water that is your birth
and your blood too.

Eating my tail

There are times in my life to which I
return like a cat scratching, licking,
worrying at an old sore, a long since
exterminated nest of fleas behind my ear.
I seem sure that if I keep poking
and rubbing that old itch will finally
be quelled.
          Or is it pre-eminent pattern I seek?
A mapmaker returning to the mountains
to pace out again the distances.
Of course, if the massacre had not
occurred in this pass, why would I care?

Some disasters alter the landscape
and realign even the roads driven
over years before.
          Yes, it is the bloody
moon of pain that gives a lurid
backlighting to this scene I peer at
suspended, a second pallid moon
beating my wings of anxiety silent
as a bat. Yet if pain gives portent
to the words spoken it denies entrance.

They sit at the table and eat. Wine
is poured, she gets up to bring
warm bread. Yellow apples are heaped
in an orange bowl whose sides reflect
candle flames. Telling a story, she takes

his hand. I know of course what she thinks
is happening and how wrong she is.

But if I opened his forehead, would I find
the violence and anger to come? Ah,
the past. It is turning out the pocket
of a jacket I wore in the garden: random
pencil nubs, plant ties, half a packet
of seeds never planted, a mummified
peach, herbs picked and forgotten—
a combination of intention and waste. Is how
it all fell down the meaning of that scene?
Yet they laugh heartily and the soup steams
and the golden apples shine like lumps of amber.

The present tears at the past as if living
were something the mind could ever hold
like water in a cup or a map in the hand.
Maps are abstractions useful for finding
whatever is actually entered on them.
Otherwise you just walk in. And through.
When you go back it's always someplace else.

Absolute zero in the brain

Penfield the great doctor did a lobotomy
on his own sister and recorded
pages of clinical observations
on her lack of initiative afterward.

Dullness, he wrote, is superseded
by euphoria at times. Slight hemi-
paresis with aphasia. The rebellious sister
died from the head down into the pages

of medical journals and Penfield founded
a new specialty. Intellectuals
sneer at moviegoers who confuse
Dr. Frankenstein with his monster.

The fans think Frankenstein is the monster.
Isn't he?

The discarded

Poor dumb animal
you go looking for him every
night in the bed he slept
in after he left mine. You
curl up there waiting.
A tremendous fuss he made
of you those months he slept
alone. Now when I call
saying you need to go to
the vet, he is furious.
The heat is shut off in that
room now and your old joints
ache as you climb the steps
stiffly looking upstairs now.
Dumb cunt. My beast,
my familiar. Come,
settle for my crowded lap
and survive him. He
has turned you too from love
into job, and resigned.

Laocoön is
the name of the figure

That sweet sinewy green nymph
eddying in curves through the grasses:
she must stop and stare at him.
Of all the savage secret creatures
he imagines stealthy in the quivering
night, she must be made to approach,
she must be tamed to love him.
The power of his wanting will turn
her from hostile dark wandering
other beyond the circle of his
campfire into his own, his flesh,
his other wanting half. To keep her
she must be filled with his baby,
weighted down.
                        Then suddenly
the horror of it: he awakens,
wrapped in the coils of the mother,
the great old serpent hag,
the hungry ravening witch who gives
birth and demands, and the lesser

mouths of the grinning children
gobbling his substance. He
must cut free.
                   An epic battle
in courts and beds and offices,
in barrooms and before the bar
and then free at last, he wanders.
There on the grassy hill, how the body
moves,
             her, the real one,
                              green
as a mayfly she hovers and he pounces.

False spring

The crocuses had stuck sharp
spikes out of the mud, opening
their striped bowls to the first
jostling bees and the pollen-colored sun.
The spears of the garlic, the small
first wrinkled leaves of mint sprang
up through the sodden oak debris.
Cardinals chased each other flaming.
The cats climbed trees and couldn't
remember how to come down. I growl
at the sky aware my anger can find
no oppressor to mark, yet I feel
squashed with the weight of snow
as it feathers down hour by hour.
It's beautiful as a tasteful Christmas
card you'd send an old professor,
but this is March. My whetted desires
turn in me like knives. Wasted thaw.
Snow mounds up while hope hisses
like blood dripping in the fireplace.

A visit from the ex

You insisted on coming.
What does he want? I muttered:
to see if the floor is swept,
if brambles have grown up over
the roof? If I've gained forty
pounds or gone bald? Curiosity
often kills its object
I learned long ago
in zoology lab, watching
the execution of frogs.

You showed me your new quartz
movement solar batteried gold
Cadillac mistress and complained
of taxes while fingering your
expenses like canker sores.
You showed me contracts, love
notes, certificates of appreciation
from governments in exile
and governments who exiled them.

Then you brought out the gifts,
packages wrapped in mauve and scarlet,
peacock, teal, amber, with bows
tied by practiced saleswomen,
posies of gilt ribbons fluttering.
Take them, you said. Enjoy.
The boxes were all empty.

It breaks

You hand me a cup of water;
I drink it and thank you pretending
what I take into me so calmly
could not kill me. We take food
from strangers, from restaurants
behind whose swinging doors flies
swarm and settle, from estranged
lovers who dream over the salad plates
of breaking the bones of our backs
with a sledgehammer.

Trust flits through the apple
blossoms, a tiny spring warbler
in bright mating plumage. Trust
relies on learned pattern
and signal to let us walk down
stairs without thinking each
step, without stumbling.

I breathe smog and pollen
and perfume. I take parts
of your body inside me. I give you
the flimsy black lace and sweat

stained sleaze of my secrets.
I lay my sleeping body naked
at your side. Jump, you shout.
I do and you catch me.

In love we open wide as a house
to a summer afternoon, every shade up
and window cranked open and doors
flung back to the probing breeze.
If we love for long, we stand like row
houses with no outer walls
on the companionable side.

Suddenly we are naked,
abandoned. The plaster of bedrooms
hangs exposed to the street, wall
paper, pink and beige skins of broken
intimacy torn and flapping.

To fear you is fearing my left
hand cut off, a monstrous crab
scaling the slippery steps of night.
The body, the lineaments of old

desire remain, but the gestures
are new and harsh. Words unheard
before are spat out grating
with the rush of loosed anger.

Friends bear back to me banner
headlines of your rewriting of our
common past. You explain me away,
a dentist drilling a tooth.
I wonder at my own trust, how absolute
it was, mortal but part of me
like the bones of my pelvis.
You were the true center of my
cycles, the magnetic north
I used to plot my wanderings.

It is not that I will not love
again or give myself into partnership
or lie naked sweating secrets
like nectar, but I will never
share a joint checking account
and when some lover tells me, *Always,*
baby, I'll be thinking, sure,
until this one too meets an heiress
and ships out. After a bone breaks
you can see in X rays
the healing and the damage.

Wind is the wall of the year

Much of what I had thought mine
essentially has fallen from me
of death, desertion, of ideas changed
conveniently as the temperature
drops and glaciers begin to creep.

The strong broad wind of autumn brushes
before it torn bags, seared apple skins,
moth wings, scraps of party velvet.
The hickory is a hard yellow scream
among maples' open raging mouths.

Lye in the wind eats the flesh from the land
till black skeletons arch against the sky,
till earth's great backbone rears, granite
picked clean of all abundance, consolation.
The road is strewn with broken ribs of branches.

Sparks spring up against the morning
devouring the last green, frying the sap.
A sheet of flame covers the day,

a cushion of haze in the bleeding afternoon,
a violent sunset over before supper.

I reach up into the sky and find
in ash of leaves, days and works, a love
I had expected to die still weaving,
dropping away to expose I must hope
some core to wait out this winter,

uncertain now if this is the winter
of my life or only a season like all
others to be entertained like a tyran-
nical guest or even enjoyed for the anatomy
it teaches as it rapidly dissects me.

IN THE MARSHES
OF THE BLOOD RIVER

More that winter ends than spring begins

Nothing stirs out of the earth,
yet the dogs are trotting in odd
pairs of schnauzer and spaniel ;
in small packs with brisk intent
they cross the streets. All over
Cambridge you can hear them barking,
sniffing each other in greeting,
raising their muzzles to drink the air
and read the gossip columns of scent.

Pigeons too are strutting on roof
beams like animate sofa pillows
puffing and cooing as they court
in the storm gutter. The old cat
crouching wary on the stoop suddenly
turns on her back and squirming
white belly up rolls on the sun
heated concrete with a sensuous shudder.

On mental corsets

Dieters talk only of weight lost
and gained, the joys of the palate
stripped down to the tang
of reading a morning scale,
zipping up pants hidden
in the back of the closet,
superiority as others gorge
on chocolate cake. The pleasures
afforded by cracking the whip
of will on one's own back
exist, surely, the smug snug
fit of being entirely in the right,
of growing healthier, stronger
while others guzzle gin and port,
while they snort, while they shoot
up, while they squander what you
are salting away. Yet recall
inflation, sudden death, flood
and fire that prohibit
the tidy enjoyment of what muscle
or gristle or gold bar that
discipline has laid as its egg.
On this the twelfth day of my diet
I would rather die satiated
than slim.

The pleasure principle

Pierrot who is the moon
the moon, a cow
the cow, a bed
with a goosedown comforter
white as nothingness.

You play with death
like a deck for solitaire,
dealing up under the eaves
where the pigeons sleep
cooing.

Who told you it wouldn't
hurt, who taught you time
ought to slide down
like children's cough
syrup, all sugar?

Damn you, with your clean
apparatus well kept
as a carving set, sticking
stupification lightning
into your arm.

I remember you pouring
and stirring the sugar
till your coffee thickened.
Trivial death: Pierrot
miming, breaks the mirror.

Let us gather at the river

I am the woman who sits by the river
river of tears
river of sewage
river of rainbows.
I sit by the river and count the corpses
floating by from the war upstream.
I sit by the river and watch the water
dwindle and the banks poke out like sore gums.
I watch the water change from green to shit brown.
I sit by the river and fish for your soul.
I want to lick it clean.
I want to turn it into a butterfly
that will weave drunkenly from orchid to rose.
I want to turn it into a pumpkin.
I want it to turn itself into a human being.

Oh, close your eyes tight and push hard
and evolve, all together now. We can
do it if we try. Concentrate
and hold hands and push.
You can take your world back
if you want to. It's an araucana
egg, all blue and green
swaddled in filmy clouds.
Don't let them cook and gobble it,
azure and jungle green egg laid
by the extinct phoenix of the universe.

Send me your worn hacks of tired themes,
your dying horses of liberation,

your poor bony mules of freedom now.
I am the woman sitting by the river.
I mend old rebellions and patch them new.

Now the river turns from shit brown to bubbling blood
as an arm dressed in a uniform
floats by like an idling log.
Up too high to see, bombers big as bowling alleys
streak over and the automated battlefield
lights up like a Star Wars pinball machine.

I am the old woman sitting by the river scolding corpses.
I want to stare into the river and see the bottom
glinting like clean hair.
I want to outlive my usefulness
and sing water songs, songs
in praise of the green brown river
flowing clean through the blue green world.

Dis-ease

With a sore back everything is hard.
The choice of a chair becomes critical.
Picking up a pencil is an operation
requiring planning, craft and caution,
a retreat executed with skill.

With a sore thumb dressing involves
the wriggling of a hooch dancer.
Why not squat on the floor and eat
out of a bowl with the cats since
that's where the food lands anyhow?

With a sore toe, every stroll
through a crowded room reeks of peril.
Strangers feel impelled to tread
on you. Every object you pass near
or touch is going to fall straight down.

Ease means the impulse blurs into the act
in one arc, with blithe unawareness.
But the wounded body calls attention to
itself, a rejected wife saying, Look at all
I used to do for you and you never noticed!

Charm for attracting wild money

You are the green of elm leaves in summer.
New you are crisp as filo dough.
Old you are soft as well worn leather.
I will rub my hands with honey
and run through the marble lobbies of banks.
I will dance for you strung like a jester
with bells of coins tinkling.

Come to me, come to me, come!
I will not keep you in a dark
trust fund. I will not chain you
to labor at a mortgage or harness
you to clanking stock issues
but I will let you wander free
as an alley cat through the city.

I will turn you out of your cage
to sing arias in the treetops.
I am not mean but foolishly kind.
You would speedily rejoin others
of your specie. Come, O green
and murmuring swarm, build
your wasp nest in my empty purse.

Of hidden taxes

Suppose those corporation spooks
had to speak frankly : we're paying you
seven fifty an hour, the usual fringes,
for a forty-hour week and your urinary
tract. We don't pay for the fifteen
years early you'll die, rather slowly.
We'll be automated by then.

Our industry is moving to your town
where we'll dump arsenic in your water.
Our executives demand fancy schools
so the tax rate will treble. We'll hang
in till all the local farmers have gone
to work for us and their farms are tract
houses. Then we'll ship out to Taiwan.

We're going to drill for oil off your shore.
Spills? We always have them. You guys
who fish and lobster might as well go
on the dole now. We loot, but then we
leave you tons of salvage. The sludge
will still be on the bottom in two
hundred years.

Suppose the President had to speak truth :
We're running a trial war over in Slit
Land, pure cocaine to the economy.
Those war-related jobs. Of course you'll

be taxed to pay off the war debt the next
twenty years. Who did you think was buying
all those bombers?

Who did you think we were making
war on anyhow? We don't even get
depreciation for you when you wear out.
We grow you to fit uniforms.
We have plans for you in overseas
demolition and population control,
and back home baby farming.

Hummingbird

Metallic apparition whirring
like a helicopter,
the golden nightingale of the Chinese
emperor breaking the sound
barrier, you seem almost
a weapon, too exquisite,
too expensive to be
useful, flashing
like a jeweled signal.
You could be a miniature
spacecraft from the Vegan
system.

Then I watch you at the orange-
salmon faces of the canna
and you are avid.
Your long beak darts,
pokes, stabs and stabs
deep in the flesh
of the flower as you sip
hovering, standing still
in the middle of the air.

Impatient, you waste no time
in going but materialize
before the bee balm, then
fast as a spark shot

from the heart of a fire
you at once thirty feet
distant drink at the phlox.

Keen at your pleasures
you zip through the garden.
Like seeing a falling
star from the corner
of my eye, as I question
the sight, it's gone.
But before the lilies
you dance probing
the last drop of nectar.

Baby at every breast,
your clean greed dazzles.
Passion has streamlined you,
no waste, no hesitation.
Every dawn hones
your hunger gleaming sharp
till death seizes
and drinks you down.

The watch

At this moment hundreds of women
a few miles from here are looking
for the same sign of reprieve, the red
splash of freedom. We run to check,
squirming through rituals of If I don't
look till two o'clock, if I skip lunch,
if I am good, if I am truly sorry,
probing, poking, hallucinating changes.
Flower, red lily, scarlet petunia
bloom for me. And some lesser number
of women in other bedrooms and bathrooms
see that red banner unfurl and mourn!
Another month, another chance missed.
Forty years of our lives, that flag
is shown or not and our immediate
and sometimes final fate determined,
red as tulips, red as poppies satin,
red as taillights, red as a stoplight,
red as dying, our quick bright blood.

The disturbance

A baby is crying at a concert.
Down the aisles of the poetry
reading, children run. Folks
scowl at the mother, pretend
collective deafness. Afterward
they say, *We felt terrible
for you*, not, *We will demand
child care next time.*

How seldom babies cry
in the university. Where
are they? Why don't fathers
bring them to work in baskets?
Have you ever studied while nursing?
Have you written a speech while cajoling
a baby raging with colic?

A visitor from Alpha Centauri
assumed humans are born full sized
after examining our public places.

Should we really just cram mother
back in the broom closet with baby
and go on with our business, grateful
for all the mothers crouching in closets
with babies chewing and weeping
talking to walls quietly
and disturbing no one else?

Toad dreams

That afternoon the dream of the toads
rang through the elms by Little River
and affected the thoughts of men,
though they were not conscious that
they heard it.—Henry Thoreau

The dream of toads: we rarely
credit what we consider lesser
life with emotions big as ours,
but we are easily distracted,
abstracted. People sit nibbling
before television's flicker watching
ghosts chase balls and each other
while the skunk is out risking grisly
death to cross the highway to mate;
while the fox scales the wire fence
where it knows the shotgun lurks
to taste the sweet blood of a hen.
Birds are greedy little bombs
bursting to give voice to appetite.
I had a cat who died of love, starving
when my husband left her too.
Dogs trail their masters across con-
tinents. We are far too busy
to be starkly simple in passion.
We will never dream the intense
wet spring lust of the toads.

Chiaroscuro

Blotter snow soaks up the dark
and quilts the shadowed leafmold park
with a fell, a pelt of light.
Dead cats and birds are decked in white
and clotted feathers, jellied eyes
are blanketed in fallen skies.

Beer can, condom, stomping grounds
are rounded into gentle mounds.
In ample curve of white one sees
what hills, what dales once were these.
Here city kids too poor for cars
thrash on the snow imprints of stars.

You're bloodfire aurora borealis,
magnetic storm on polar ice
while traffic sounds encroach like malice
on all you'll taste of paradise.

Warm couples coiling lapped in drift
can your tight parentheses
keep in the fever? My cure was swift,
O dark children under bone white trees.

A snarl for loose friends

Many who say friend,
friend, clutch their balls like prayers
for fear something of themselves
may break loose and get away.

Many who mumble love,
love keep an eye fixed for the fire
ladder, the exit hatch and at the first
sign of trouble do not hang around to chat.

Many who talk of community
called the real estate agent last night
and the papers are drawn up to sell their land
to a nuclear power plant that shows dirty movies.

Don't count your friends by their buttons
until you have seen them pushed a few times.

Jill in the box

All the women rusted closed, who peeped
at sunlight through drawn curtains.
All the women with headaches snaking
up through their spine twisting, writhing
and knocking finally on the inside of the skull
like something pounding on a door
to be let out. Women who saw the sky
only through slats, through a high barred
shutter, through dust on factory windows,
never were allowed to dare. To seize
adventure, to push through hunger to knowledge.
Their blood was blooming like roses secretly.
Their eyes were bruised by irises, by lilies
waving their bright and fragrant organs
in the air. All the women whose feet
were twisted half off, whose ankles
were hobbled. Who had babies
put into them in the dark like mushrooms.
Their longings spurted electric fountains
from the severed head while their bodies
wore down, decaying like old sponges.

The nation bristles still with busy people
who long to cut off women's hands and feet,
forbid us to bloom rampant and scarlet
as a hedge of rambling roses and thorns,
who want us to fear roaming and soaring,
who want us never to dance under the moon,
who want to forbid us to bare our breasts
to the sun and walk among our tomatoes
simply naked as cats.

Down at the bottom of things

In the marshes of the blood river
frogs blurt out their grocery lists
of lust, and some frogs croak poems.
In the brackish backwaters of the psyche
the strong night side of our nature
develops its food chain. I do believe
that in corporate board rooms, in bank
offices, in the subcommittees of Congress,
senators with oil bribes easing their way
toward power act from greed, yes,
but petty hatreds flash swarming thick
as piranhas in their murky speeches, and around
their deals musty resentments circle
buzzing like fat dirty horseflies.

In the salty estuary of the blood river
small intermittent truths dart
in fear through the eel grass, and the nastier
facts come striding, herons stabbing
with long bills yet graceful when they rise in heavy
flight. Here we deal with the archaic base
of advertising slogans and bureaucratic
orders that condemn babies to kwashiorkor,
here on the mud flats of language. Our duty
rises red as the rusty moon, waxing
and waning surely but always returning.

Here where the salty fluids of the blood
meet the renewal of fresh water streaming
from the clouds soaked through the grasses,
down runoff ditches, wandering through brown

meanders of stream; here where the ocean
turns on its elbow muttering and begins
to heave back on itself, whispering
its rise in all the little fiddler crab
burrows, through all the interstices
of tidal grass, we read the news
in minute flotsam of the large
catastrophes out at sea and upriver.
The oil slicks, the wrecks, the sewage
tainted, the chemicals dumped in the stream
we taste here clamlike as we strain
the waters to prophesy in frogs' tongues.

Working, we curl cheek to the pulse
of the earth breathing, the mother of life
entering us and withdrawing twice daily.
A marsh smells like sex and teems
with tiny life that all the showier
big creatures of the shallow sea
fatten on. Here the only decision
that presents itself is to see, to watch,
to taste, to listen, to know and to say,
all with care as the heron stalks probing,
all with care as the crab scuttles into the safety
of burrow, all with care as the kingfisher
watches, one way the fish, the other way,
the hawk. To survive saying, to say again
and again, here in the rich soup of creation,
in the obscure salty pit where the rhythms
of life repeat and renew, and the cost
of greed is etched in poison on every cell.

Out of the hospital Peter

Out of the hospital Peter examines his garden.
"You haven't been watering the squash enough,"
he announces, secretly pleased. In our absence
the trees should not topple, the lilies
should not wither black with anthracnose,
the tomatoes should not be chewed to the stems
by the sea monster shape of the horned worm
but there should be some damage, some visible
tangible pinchable tarnish of missing.

That satisfies. The invalid shuffles
reaching for and missing a grasshopper
whose teeth have sieved the strawberry
leaves. Nods at the sun-colored swinging
bells of the daylilies, who nod back,
healthy, splendid, multiplying even
in drouth. The person who has recently
sunk in that slime cold pool and drifted
down and deep where the faint light blackens
and the heart shudders along like a failing
submarine is comforted also by the bright
vigor of the daylilies blazing in the noon
making new flowers for each new day.

Gardens draw the healing as they boil
with life and death in soothing colors.
The gardener knows you win some (seven
pounds of snap beans on Sunday, five
on Tuesday) and some you lose (the apples
wizened already in July, worm raddled)

and some go on heedless, indifferent
to our scrutiny, to set flowers, make
seeds and sigh into compost again.
You can play god, play nature, abdicate,
philosophize, set up experiments, enter
into relationships with your plants,
sculpt with bushes and shrubs,
or you can sit in the freckled shade
watching the zucchini swell as the corpuscles
swarm like bees and the tissues rebuild
themselves like lettuce after picking.

The working writer

I admire you to tantrums they say,
you're so marvelously productive,
those plump books in litters
like piglets. You're an example
to us all they say
but not of what.

Then the comments light on my face
stinging like tiny wasps,
busy-busy, rush-rush, such a steamy
pressured life. Why don't
you take a day or week off
when I visit? I spend July
at the beach myself. August
I go to Maine. Martinique
in January. I keep in shape
Thursdays at the exercise salon.
Every morning I do yoga for two
hours; it would mellow you.
Then I grind wheat berries
for bread, weave macrame hammocks
and whip up a fluffy mousseline dress.
Oh, you buy your clothes.

I just don't know how you live
with weeds in the living room,
piles of papers so high the yellow
snow on top is perennial. Books

in the shower, books in bed,
a freezer full of books.
You need a cleaning lady or two.
They cost so little.
I saw a bat in the bedroom
last night, potatoes flowering
behind the toilet.

My cats clean the house, I say.
I have them almost trained.
I work myself.
In winter we dig the potatoes.
All year we eat the books.

Right Wing Mag: a found poem

If you turn this page, You
and Your Loved Ones may starve.
Economic Dunkirk, it is coming!
Reap spectacular profits
while others are losing theirs.
Congressman Larry McDonald
identified 120 socialists in Congress.
The Handgun has become the symbol of freedom.
Fighting both death and taxes with a unique
mix of economic and religious commentary.
I have used my own personal distiller every day
for ten years without service needed.
Dedicated to the support of gold.

Free catalog for Christian Patriots.
Shyster zionist courts. You high rollers
pay attention now. Imagine a contest to the death
between two individuals who are in the same
part of the forest. Three little
known tax loopholes. This elite
security force offers counterterrorist.
Exciting body massage. Investment diamonds
won't set off airport metal detectors.
You can't eat gold. Store dehydrated
and freeze-dried survival foods.
The only safe that's *really* safe
is one nobody can find.

It weeps away

I break the egg on the rim of the iron pan
and in the seep of albumin,
in the plop of heavier gold
marbled around the red eye, run out
the bronze feathers of the cock,
the tireless pecking and clucking
of the barred hen.
                    Thus I lay
for five days with the fever rising
and sweated my strength into the quilt.
The poem I cupped in my eggshell
skull bled out.

The world in the year 2000

It will be covered to a depth of seven
inches by the little white plastic
chips at once soft and repellent
to the touch and with the ability
to bounce like baby beach balls
under the table and under the radiator.
They come in boxes with toasters,
with vitamin pills, with whatever
you order, as packing material : they
will conquer the world. They are
doing it already beginning
with my kitchen.

Very late July

July in the afternoon, the sky
rings, a crystal goblet without a crack.
One gull passes over mewing for company.
A tiger swallowtail hovers near magenta
phlox, while a confetti cloud
of fritillaries covers the goldenglow.
The sun lowers a helmet of flame
over my skull till my brain cooks
yellow as chicken skin. Beside me
half under the tent of my skirt, my cat
blinks at the day, content watching,
allowing the swallowtail to light
within paw reach, purring too softly
to be heard, only the vibration from his
brown chest buzzing into my palm.
Among the scarlet blossoms of the runner
beans twining on their tripods
the hummingbird darts like a jet fighter.
Today in think tanks, the data analysts
not on vacation are playing war games.
A worker is packing plutonium by remote
control into new warheads. An adviser
is telling a president as they golf,
we could win it. July without a crack
as we live inside the great world egg.

For the Furies

Behold the man who produces movies
evacuated from his impacted dreams
in which a woman is raped and enjoys it
as you might enjoy an electric saw
taking off your thumb. May he go to jail
for back parking ticket violations
and be had by a platoon of three-hundred-
pound bullies who call him cute when he screams.
May his ass be sold for butts.

See the man with the square jaw
and regimental stripe tie from the utility
who explains on TV how safety standards
for nuclear power are unreasonably high;
how low level radiation is good for growing
things (causing parts to grow secretly
and fast), good for people especially
if they have excess hair. May that man
prove sterile, his wife leave him for
a geneticist with lots of hair and may
he die at his leisure of leukemia.

Here's a man who designs cigarette ads
showing that all slim long-legged women
with blond hair toting tennis rackets
and all virile men who ride bucking
mountains bareback are never without a butt.
Then working class kids start smoking

at twelve to hack their lungs out at forty.
He will wake with a deep cough this morning.
I know how the blood tastes when you choke
it up; that boiling lead melting your lungs;
a granite boot that crushes your chest
as you fight for air, drowning in bed.

A curse on the man who owns slum buildings.
It's not cost effective to fumigate, to fix
the halls, the stairs, the doors, the windows.
It's cheaper to bribe city inspectors.
He lives in a high rise on the water
and hides in a maze of paper corporations.
His tenants breathe garbage and scuttle
through traps of hallways dark as mines.
Tonight as he strolls by the old wharves
renovated for ferny bars, brokers
and Danish importers, an army of rats
will slip from the old stones, surround,
nip and eat him. It will take them
hours to reach the fatty liver.

A curse on his business partner who dwells
in a perfect barely postrevolutionary
war mansion on ten acres outside Concord.
He finances his buildings by a spot of arson;
then ho! for a singles condominium.
The Puerto Rican woman weeping in the street

for her dead baby can always have another,
if she hasn't yet been sterilized.
All I ask is that at the big barbecue
with his bankers he drink well of the martinis
before he goes to light the fire.
Let him forget to drop and roll.

Consider the chemical company president
who dumps PCB in the river, killing
the fish at once and the children twenty
years later. The workers start failing
with that weariness that never eases,
first pain in the head, then the chest.
He makes people choose between jobs
with cancer and no jobs with hunger.
May his wife take a lover and feed
her husband arsenic daily, by gradual
doses. Each day he will rouse from bed
less hot to wheel and deal. Colleagues
suggest a vacation *If you can't cut
the mustard*. Let her weep at his grave
and smile when the will is read.

Watch the contrails of the generals who play
war games and long for the real thing,
who know that when the fire storm swirls
through cities melting girders and bones,
vaporizing flesh, when millions crawl
flayed and starving through suburban rubble,
they will be sampling the caviar inventory

74

in the bunker under the mountain. Let the good
green arthropods of the Space Police
come and banish them to a planet in its bronze
age, where generals have to fight in single
combat with sharp axes and dullish swords.

We are fruit flies who swarm under glass
in the laboratory, on whom scientists test
mutations. They are our careless owners.
We copulate, feed and stretch our brief
flimsy wings, uncomprehending who sends
our plagues of filth and boils, who leaches
calcium from our children's crisp bones,
who robs us of years, who rifles our genes.

Cursing is the puffery of the weak
who cannot put in a good word to the D.A.,
who cannot summon their senator on the line
to remind of donations past and lurking,
or order our foundation to sponsor
justice this year; who cannot threaten
the bank with moving our funds into yen.

Those who steal from the poor their safety,
their kidneys, their colons, their lungs,
their friendly web of neighbors and stores,
their sleep, their respect, their history and future,
their hard-used bodies, steal by fiat
with clean hands and consciences that ring
when tapped like clear thin crystal goblets

for their wine. They are good men
who give to charity and join appropriate
organizations, coddle their children
whom they send to the best private schools.
For them, murder is ordering a pair of ski
boots from a catalog. The dead, the mangled
are faceless others removed like rock
from a hill the superhighway blasts through.

Crimes against the father are punished here,
crimes against the State, authority, banks,
crimes against property. But crimes against
the mother are honored, paid in gold.
Weave connections, weave a spider web
around them, weave the cloth in which we all
are threads, weave connections and weave again
closer, finer. The old weird sisters
were too poor to own more than one eye:
fates, gorgons, furies, expanding to muses,
contracting into the round moon. Justice
of the many is wishes, the slow connection
weaving like a net, a strong net
woven of dreams and cursing, to catch sharks.

DIGGING IN

The annealing

We begin in a burning house.
We begin by bandaging each
other's wounds. We begin by
holding each other in night
streaked by tracer bullets.

I hike toward you with pain
riding my back like a grandfather,
my blood burning its oil
from the slaughtered
leviathans of lost years.

Collision of choice and accident,
we are thrust at each other,
abandoned animals who crawl
into a culvert to share
shelter and bodily warmth.

With the stench of smoke,
webs of soot in our hair,
nonetheless we carry
each embers of a hearth
fire we'll lay together.

In the ruins we raise
a new house, round
as a sleeping cat and founded
without evasion, without denial
on the bedrock of death.

Three loser's poems

1. The account is closed

Sometimes in loss a tension
loosens in the chest or in
the mind. You bribed her
to love you, proving every
week what you had proved the week
before on tallies that never
matched, a checking account
with a hidden leak. You
were ripe to be discarded,
a coat once favored, hanging
in the back of the closet. Yet
one woman's discard is another's
rummaged treasure. This ending
is a scene you rehearsed nightly
growling like a dog that fights
in sleep, his hackles raised
as he curls before the fire.
Every time you left her door
you peopled her space with lovers
usurping table and bed where you slept
between her and the clammy
sweating wall of your anxiety.
Your fears have come true
and you will outlive them.

2. What does pain remind you of?

In every loss
all the old pains resonate
like arthritic joints groaning,
like croaking corns in the rain.
The first rejection at the end
of infancy and every scorn
and sneer and betrayal moulder
like canned goods gone bad
in the root cellar of memory.
They seethe with fermentation
bulging their lids.
                    In dreams
I die and wake shuddering
and the morning breaks
like a skim of ice
under my weight.

3. After the frost

After the first October
frost the tomato plants stand
charred, the eggplants wither,
the marigolds rattle their dried

and shrunken hairy heads.
Yet the lettuce still rounds itself,
the cabbages are fat as babies,
the carrots raise their ferns.
We have less work to do; mostly
we gather in what survives. Half
your life you say is dead.
Yet the hardier half thrives
and will feed you still,
oh my love, as we scurry
like field mice among the hard
white ribs of winter.

The world comes back
like an old cat

Slowly the topography emerges, a pile
of thatch from the marsh, a mounded up
rosebush, a pitchfork forgotten several
blizzards ago, rusty tines upthrust from
where its handle froze to the earth,
rows of parsnip and leek still growing,
pellets of owl victims, skull of a vole,
the sharp ears of the crocus: the sun licks
the world into being frenzied with detail
the snow glossed over in its beautiful
monotonous frieze of blue and white marble.

Trying to attract your attention
without being too obvious

I:
I am placing
placing my body before you
like a bowl of apples
like a bunch of grapes.
I:
where I am:
I am inside waiting.
I am the fierce hollow.
I am the wanting
this body grows around.

Touch

Suddenly the sun touches the top
of my head through the window over
the sickly basil plant sucked by
white fly and I am startled and place
my hand on my scalp, hot as the stove
top when the oven is on : sun
you have zigzagged your way up
the steep chiaroscuro slope of winter.
For months I have not had to raise
my eyes to give you that quick
blink of hello. Though the garden
is blue with snow and icicles
bend the pines, you are on your way
back. No more darkness at three
thirty. The afternoons are ample.
Brighter and fatter every day, burning
apple, lion-colored rose, already you
are freeing the creek from the ice,
the crocus from the soil and me from
my desk and the winter cocoon of fat
I will burn like a torch for your rising.

Death of the Hungarian
hot pepper bush

While I was quarreling with you
my shiny green upright hot pepper
plant died. All through our tedious
mutual vivisection it was wilting,
all the zest and vigor it crams
into long fingerling peppers like a bush
of traffic signals, first green,
then yellow, then ultimate blistering
red, ebbing along the drooping
branches, the crackling leaves.

No more fresh Hungarian hot peppers
in the snow. I mourn the lover
cleared out and the plant dead
but I focus on guilt. The bush
died at my elbow all afternoon.

Guilt is veneer to lay over pain,
stoking the ego till it steams
the eyes, fogs up the inside
of the head. Guilt is the godlike
fix, breeding analysis and the self
as a consuming hobby. Tend it

like a fig tree in the living
room and it will repay you with total
protection from anyone living.

Let me mourn the hot pepper
and the hot lover gone off in a spout
of scalding words. Let me collect
seeds from the last peppers,
weep all night and plot an accidental
meeting next Tuesday. Burnt
and chilled I chew my pain
like horseradish root. It's real
and may go on for a while in its season
like the falling snow.

The surf of joy pounding

Now is the nova just bursting,
the moving flood at crest,
the tall waves leaping and crashing
with a slither of icy joy radiating
out to the farthest nerve
in the ultima thule of cold toes.

I am an ocean of skin undulating.
We are wave upon wave splashing and driving,
porpoises arching and lewd,
whales slabbing our massive tails
as we dive for the deepest dark.
We are seas meeting seas over and under
interpenetrating our salty wet
currents, heaving rich and phosphorescent.

I walk through the office aisles
of my work past the in and out boxes,
past the messengers and the computer links
and on my retina the moon flickers,
humping us into flood tide attacking
the drab land and then flattening
us peaceful again in ebb.
I am this elastic container of rational
discourse and shopping lists
while the ocean roars and breaks
on the inside of my forehead.

Why in Toronto?

My other flesh, this is the third
annual feast of the rising of our moon
of content and here I am stuck in the air
like a kite the wind shreds.

I can no more control what's happening
than a torn newspaper splatted against
a wire fence. My thwarted desires beat
on the airplane window like a mad chimp

on the glass wall of its tiny cage
in a stingy zoo. We land, a die cast.
Past midnight in a city where I have no
business I spend the night in a motel

bed courtesy of Air Canada and their lack
of interest in our affairs.
The third anniversary of the end
of loneliness I am alone.

The back pockets of love

Your toes:
  modest stalagmites
    sticking up in the ice caves
      of the winter bed.

Your toes:
  succulent mushrooms,
    stumpy chimney pots
      rising in their row.

Wee round faces
  anonymous as nuns,
    callused, worn as coolies
      aging in their traces.

Small fry,
  wriggling moonbeam
    minnows escaped from the dark
      traps of your shoes.

Pipsqueak puppets,
  piglets nosing,
    soft thimbles, dumpy
      sofa pillows of flesh.

Love dwells in the major caves of the psyche,
 chewing on the long bones of the limbs of courage,

the great haunches of resolution,
sucking the marrow bones, caves lit
by the lasting flames of the intellect,

but love cherishes too the back pockets,
the pencil ends of childhood fears,
the nose picking and throbbing sweet tooth,
the silly hardworking toes that curl
now blamelessly as dwarf cats
in the warm covers of the sweet
tousled nest of mutual morning bed.

In search of scenery

The copper beech arches over
us, stout grey limbs supple and smooth
as our flesh, fluttering coarse
leaves black in the moonlight but
red in the pool of lamplight as pollen
from the heart of the lily whose scent
thickens the soft air of summer
from its bed by the house wall.

We have crept into this garden,
embrace on this lawn as the tree
not ours whispers its silken hair
overhead. My beeches are adolescent
saplings and when I stand near them
I dread caterpillars. My lilies
demand staking. My garden groans
for water as the cauliflowers wilt
their elephant leaves and ravenous
slugs gnaw the cabbages to lace.

To enjoy scenery gracious, compliant
as lovers desire, backgrounds that play

soft violins, we must not possess.
We creep away from chores to landscapes.
Our soil utters threats of a creditor,
our trees mutter complaints and grocery lists.
Only the woods of strangers murmur
sensually of velvet beds on the night
like a cat that greets you companionably
in the street, rubbing at your leg
before padding off on the scent of courtship
under a moon that rises a mint fresh penny
full, round and copper as this arching beech.

Mornings in various years

1.

To wake and see the day piled up
before me like dirty dishes: I have
lived years knitting a love that
he would unravel, as if Penelope
spent every night making a warm
sweater that Odysseus would tear
in his careless diurnal anger.

2.

Waking alone I would marshal my tasks
like battalions of wild geese to bear me
up on the wings of duty over
the checkered fields of other lives.
Breakfast was hardest. I would trip
on ghostly shards of broken
domestic routines that entangled
my cold ankles as the cats yowled
to be fed, and so did I.

3.

I wake with any two cats, victors
of the nightly squabble of who
sleeps where, and beside me, you

your morning sleepyhead big as a field
pumpkin, sleep caught in your fuzzy
hair like leaves. The sun pours in
sweet as orange juice or the rain licks
the windows with its tongue or the snow
softly packs the house in cotton batting
or the wind rocks us on its bellows.
When we wake we move toward each other.
This opal dawn glows from the center
as we both open our eyes and reach out
asking, are you there? You! You're
there, the unblemished day before us
like a clean white ironstone platter
waiting to be filled.

The name I call you

A stained glass window pieced
from broken gutter bottles,
pain and jagged edges, loss and waste,
the refuse of city lives jangling:
now the mellow colors dapple our skin
and the emblem is the sun.

Already we have slept in thirty
beds together, learning how to share
the shaggy underbelly of the night,
learning how to sleep in each other's
arms, learning how to follow dreams
down the whirlpool of eyes
the color of night and day, of wolf
and water, of bark and leaf.
Every week has its seasons of plenty
and lack, its droughts and its monsoons,
its small Julys and its miniature Februarys.

Sometimes we coil together, kittens
who at once suckle and suck, both
drawing sweet rich strength from the other,
both giving, both taking. Sometimes
we leap from ledge to ledge, scanning
new territory, tearing open
new insights, traveling
like ocelots, big cats
who swim, hunt paired,

share all their tasks, guard
the other's flank.

For three years we have loved, now well,
now badly, now a love of honey and fire,
now of bone and rust, now of pick handles
entwined with red roses. I hold my breath
like a candle in the wind
trotting toward you, eager now
as the first night, the first month,
the first summer and fall and winter.
Love is work. Love is pleasure. Love
is studying. Love is holding and
letting go without going away.
Love is returning and turning
and rebuilding and building new.
Love is words mating like falcons a mile
high, love is work growing
strong and blossoming like an apple tree,
love is two rivers that flow together,
love is our minds stretching out webs
of thought and wonder and argument slung
across the flesh or the wires of distance,
love is the name I call you.

The West Main
Book Store chickens

Always a shock:
like biting into a waxy golden
apple that shines like the harvest moon
and finding it mush.
In diners, in restaurants squatting at the end of motels
breathing liquory air, I order eggs.
The first bite lies on my tongue
rubbery as a bathing cap.

O eggs of Joanna's chickens,
your yolks are yellow as April sunshine.
Yellow as daffodil trumpets.
Sweet as sweet butter.
Your whites are clear and fragrant,
bowls of shad blossoms.

Joanna's chickens all have names.
They can fly. You look at them
and they cock their heads and look back.
Their manure feeds my cucumbers.
Gemma picks them up to talk to, hen
tucked under her arm like a fat puppy.
One bronze rooster gleams.
Quiches tender as rose petals,
mayonnaise you could grow fat admiring:
real chickens lay real eggs.

Homecoming

As I drive home through the floating
sheets of rain, blowing like gauze
the occasional light whitens,
the red eyes of doggy cars
watch me as they run
backwards, always the same
distance ahead so I feel
myself hang motionless
straining helplessly forward
with my foot pressed down hard
through the whooshing dark.

Two peach trees

First one blooms quietly and earlier, white
blossoms like the small roses of old
multiflora growing around abandoned pastures
in a high impassible tangle that hints
of Sleeping Beauty: but before barbed wire
those roses held cattle from the corn and the road.
Then the other tree opens, double and brilliant,
shocking against the soft pinks, pale yellows,
the shad whites of spring, tropical fuchsia
burning and caressing the eyes starved
for color. On sunny days bees drone
among the limbs. Then the fingers of the leaves
uncoil, elegant, languid, drooping.

The peaches among them are fuzzballs the size
of the nail on your pinkie. Then forever they
hang hard and green and stubborn. Thunk
they drop on your head, wooden bullets.
You kick them in the grass like croquet
balls as the summer swells. When will they
ever blush? You must have rain earlier
and later you must not have rain. They rot
in rain, they rot in fog, they fall off
in high winds. Spores of brown fungus
discolor your dreams.

Now they are ripe, one tree of big yellow
peaches the color of late afternoon sun
at the beach, when it is golden on your skin
slanting across the sandbar, when even the pines
on the bluff shine red. All things discover

100

their secret ruddiness. The other bears
small white peaches you can eat whole
juicier than kisses. Season of canning cuts,
scalding kettles, rows of sterilized jars.

Peaches, peaches, you taste like the flesh
of a lover, the furry skin, the heft,
the sweet gush of you, the utterly ripe
sunwarmed fragility, the scent filling my head
like saxophones, lingering, brandy on the tongue.
Golden and ivory, sand colors, colors of dune,
peaches of the sun and peaches of the moon,
black-eyed susan and ox-eyed daisy fruit,
round as the heads of downy infants, round
as quail in the snow. The trees are not mates
but self fertile. Yet loving only themselves
they bear generously their load of little
round bellies of honey and wine
satisfying in all seasons.

Woody's wool

It's a holly bush
vigorous under the snow.
It's a forest of curly kale,
a crinkly savoy cabbage
turned inside out. It's curls
from the foreheads of little
brown goats kicking up their hooves
among the scorched rocks,
with bells on their necks.
It's a halo exploding.
It's a dome of feathers.
It's an anemone of velvet.
It's the upturned belly
of a rolling spring lamb.
It's a grass field that dropped acid.
It's a cloud settled down.
It's pubic, over your eyes.
It's something to get lost in.
I do.

Snow, snow

Like the sun on February ice dazzling;
like the sun licking the snow back
roughly so objects begin to poke through,
logs and steps, withered clumps of herb;
like the torch of the male cardinal
borne across the clearing from pine
to pine and then lighting among the bird
seed and bread scattered; like the sharp
shinned hawk gliding over the rabbit
colored marsh grass, exulting
in talon-hooked cries to his larger mate;
like the little pale green seedlings sticking
up their fragile heavy heads on white stalks
into the wide yellow lap of the pregnant sun;
like the sky of stained glass the eye seeks
for respite from the glitter that makes the lips
part; similar to all of these pleasures
of the failing winter and the as yet unbroken
blue egg of spring is our joy as we twist
and twine about each other in the bed
facing the window where the sun plays
the tabla of the thin cold air
and the snow sings soprano
and the emerging earth drones bass.

Still waters

The pond is a silvered mirror that cuts
you in half, giving you four arms,
two heads and no legs at all as you wade
provoking ripples and then stop, appearing
trapped in heavy dark water under
a violet sky.
The water is warm as feathers.
Voices spear across the pond clearer
than through a motel wall: *I didn't!*
You did. You lie all the time, they
argue, voices like glass bells. When you
begin to swim, you break the mirror.
Your arm rises and falls like a snake
striking. Your feet kick fountains.
Swimming more slowly, less competently
after you I am suddenly afraid. The pond
seems a large opened mouth
that might close on you, that might swallow
us to separate darknesses. Treading
water I call, *Woody, Woody* after you.
The voices of our doubles, the quarreling
lovers in the darkness under the trees,
fall still. I hear the thrashing of your feet
near, then cease. Under water you seize
my legs. We hug, splash back to shore.
Across the black soup, they are swatting
each other with words again, but it doesn't
matter. A woman in love goes through
luminous rings of terror that pop
like soap bubbles silently. I lose you
and find you all day and all night.

Song like a thin wire

Not even the female mosquito
whining its song of lust
over your pillow wants you
as desperately as I, with only
my tires whining on the treadmill
of pavement through the galloping
dark as my hands clutch hard
on the wheel, waiting to close
upon you.

A key to common lethal fungi

What rots it is taking
for granted. To assume what
is given you is laid on like the water
that rushes from the faucet singing
when you turn the tap. Wait
till the reservoir goes dry
to learn how precious are those
clear diamond drops.

We hunt our lovers like deer
through the thorny thickets and after
we have caught love we start
eating it to the bone.
We use it up in hamburgers
complaining of monotony.

We walk all over the common miracles
without bothering to wipe our feet.
Then we wonder why we need more
and more salt to taste our food.

My old man, my old lady, my
ball and chain: listen, even the cat
you found starving in the alley

who purrs you to sleep dancing
with kneading paws in your hair
will vanish if your heart closes its fist.

Habit's fine dust chokes us.
As in a city the streetlights
and neon signs prevent us from viewing
the stars, so the casual noise, the smoke
of ego turning over its engine blinds
us till we can no longer see past
our minor needs to the major constellations
of the ram, the hunter, the swan
that guide our finite gaze
through the infinite dark.

Ascending scale

Climbing a long open flight of sandstone steps
shallow, interminable under a sun beating the gong
       of my skull,
as if to a sacrificial platform topping an Aztec pyramid
here on the campus of a southern university in August
for a writers' conference, I met myself descending.

The flat dark eyes of a woman a few years older caught
me on brambles, tearing at my orderly advance
       with briefcase,
the scarlet gauze of my new dress floating around me
like love. I winced at her disheveled anger, the heat
bruising her, the want shining out in waves of black light.

She arrived early ; she is staying an extra day ; she rushes
from workshop to reception, while I operate on the end of
       a long
elastic twanging its overextension. Always rushing back
to you, always a little annoyed to be elsewhere, I work hard
and shake hands with a calm surrounding a vacuum.

If I lose you like a gold earring in a motel room,
if we misplace each other like a book gone out of print,
if we exhaust love with carelessness, forget to change
       the oil

and let it burn out, haul resentments from elsewhere home
      like mean
relatives who move in and take over, then we will fail

as everyone expects. Loss creates the sad woman I
      met climbing
who raked my face for answers that will never sort. That
      wanting
self would be available salted like nuts on a table, gracious
and needy, what the students imagine they want. I know
      better.
The strength they covet and use is rooted in the plentitude
      of love.

Digging in

This fall you will taste carrots
you planted, you thinned, you mulched,
you weeded and watered. You don't
know yet they will taste like yours,
not others, not mine.
This earth is yours as you love it.

We drink the water of this hill
and give our garbage to its soil.
We haul thatch for it and seaweed.
Out of it rise supper and roses
for the bedroom and herbs
for your next cold.

Your flesh grows out of this hill
like the maple trees. Its sweetness
is baked by this sun. Your eyes

have taken in sea and the light leaves
of the locust and the dark bristles
of the pine.

When we work in the garden you say
that now it feels sexual, the plants
pushing through us, the shivering
of the leaves. As we make love
later the oaks bend over us,
the hill listens.

The cats come and sit on the foot
of the bed to watch us.
Afterwards they purr.
The tomatoes grow faster and the beans.
You are learning to live in circles
as well as straight lines.

The doe

On Bound Brook Island on December
24th, the air is mild and the sky
sags gently like a wet blanket
with promise of snow. Then
from a thicket of holly she bursts
leaping with her white tail
rising and dipping. Almost
the length of the valley to the bay
she runs before settling
in a copse. Poor cover here.
In summer she would only jump
the brook and sprint a few yards.
Thus the solstice blesses us
with her surviving the hunters
and the leap of our own hearts
that thud with her hooves as she bounds.

On New Year's Day

Bless this my house under the pitch pines
where the cardinal flashes and the kestrels hover
crying, where I live and work with my lover
Woody and my cats, where the birds gather
in winter to be fed and the squirrel dines
from the squirrel-proof feeder. Keep our water
bubbling up clear. Protect us from the fire's
long teeth and the lashing of the hurricanes
and the government. Please, no foreign wars.
Keep this house from termites and the bane
of quarreling past what can be sweetly healed.
Keep our cats from hunters and savage dogs.
Watch with care over Woody splitting logs
and mostly keep us from our sharpening fear
as we skate over the ice of the new year.

A private bestiary

I want us to be dolphins
together whose whole envelope
of skin sensitive as nipples
crinkles in joy, who roll over
and over borne up in the cradle
of water, sensuous, grinning at play.

I want to fly as falcons with you,
mating high in the blazing air
while the winds carry us scudding
then let us drop a thousand feet
elevator down, our talons locked
while the sun screams spurting blood.

I want to coil as snakes with you
twining slow and inseparable,
cold and patient as oak trees,
with our dry diamond-patterned skin
rubbing, rasping as we slither under
and round like knotted silk rope.

I want to be snails together, happy
hermaphrodites who approach

and approach and approach and then
make love, each lover and loved, active
and passive day long, coming
in long billowing orgasms like clouds.

I want to mate as dinosaurs,
hot blooded, furred, feathered and big
as roller coasters, chasing each other
roaring among the jungle furniture,
uprooting trees, panting steam
while turtle shells rattle like castanets.

On your skin I read bestiaries
by braille. In our bed we curl, stones
sleeping in our mountainside, fossils
locked inside; we open scarlet fragrant
petal by petal from the gold stamened center;
lion meets lion while lamb greets lamb.

In which she begs (like everybody else) that love may last

The lilac blooms now in May,
our bed awash with its fragrance,
while beside the drive, buds
of peony and poppy swell
toward cracking, slivers of color
bulging like a flash of eye
from someone pretending to sleep.
Each in its garden slot, each
in its season, crocus gives way
to daffodil, through to fall
monkshood and chrysanthemum.
Only I am the wicked rose
that wants to bloom all year.
I am never replete with loving
you. Satisfaction
makes me greedy. I want
to blossom out with my joy of you
in March, in July, in October.
I want to drop my red red
petals on the hard black ice.

ELEMENTARY ODES

What goes up

A photograph of an eagle just setting down
on the ice of Quabbin, pinions outspread:
look a winter storm in the eye.

Jack Swedberg when a construction worker
at Quabbin saw a bald eagle one day,
first encounter with the fierce queen of winds

and bought a camera. Conversion.
The raptor seized him into art, carried
off to his vocation like a rabbit.

The local hawks drag awe from me,
a giant reel of wire unwinding up the sky,
me, a fish on the bottom of my pond, hooked.

The ocean of air: a phrase that lacks
vividness till you fly. The big jets
ride the long waves up where air thins,

but oceans are wet all through. Call it
an aureole of air, like the mane of white
fire around the lion head sun in total eclipse.

The black blue of the sky from a high
altitude plane is cold and daunting.
I cannot look long. It blinds me.

We are feathered with air, downed

with it. Air is our second skin.
It enters us like a lover, or we die.

We call the sky blue that each season
repaints, as often in pigeon grey,
wet granite, pearl mist; its midnight

velvet, gauze or marble. One time I saw
the sky curdle ominous, split pea soup,
as I stood dumb in the Chicago street

hearing my mother say, *Then the sky
turned green in Ohio*. The funnel reached
its paw down, and I ran like hell.

Over a neon strip the sky is lit red
with a thousand bonfires. The sulphurous
brown grey of the sky in New York

hangs into the street like a sagging belly.
The white sky of winter in the mountains
freezes to the slope, one blinding bank.

Sky of summer drought banging brass
gongs. Sky of thunderstorms slamming oaken
doors. Sky of fog fallen, tearing on pines.

Yet you are the intimate element, in
and out of our bodies all day, feeding
us quietly, stoking our little fires.

You give yourself to us, but we cannot
give ourselves to you. We are too
gross for your thinness to sustain.

Only the creatures whose bodies you
have shaped can fly: the hummingbird
who spins sunlight into jewels.

The spring azures light among puddles
on the sand road as if the rain
had brought down shreds of sky.

The monarch rising among the milkweed
is colored like a pumpkin moon. A cloud
of floating exclamation points:

fritillaries. Night raises
the small furred umbrellas of the bats,
dada jokes squeaking, toys on wires.

We dirty you and the trees clean you.
We spend you and the trees grow you
green again with oxygen.

The sea breathes wind. Here on this
sandbar we fear the storm but relish it.
It kills. It tears down. It resculpts

the shore, building new bars and cutting

through lagoons, drowning islands, digging
up wrecks while breaking ships in two.

It rips at the cliffs till the summer
houses built of glass slide over. Jaegers
stand bemused in the marsh, birds of the deep.

The storm is vaster than imagination.
My house rocks on its waves moaning.
Branches lop off with sharp reports.

The pines lash double in the tumult.
Waterfalls hurtle dashing from the eaves.
The joints of the walls crack. The roof

whistles. Death brushes dark wings
against our shoulders but flies on
heavily, a great crow on the tempest.

Afterward we venture out to confront
an altered world. Whatever is torn down,
whatever is fallen, whatever is smashed,

the hope banked low in us as we step
into the washed air, flares up yellow
and hot and leaps, as we live and breathe.

The common living dirt

The small ears prick on the bushes,
furry buds, shoots tender and pale.
The swamp maples blow scarlet.
Color teases the corner of the eye,
delicate gold, chartreuse, crimson,
mauve speckled, just dashed on.

The soil stretches naked. All winter
hidden under the down comforter of snow,
delicious now, rich in the hand
as chocolate cake: the fragrant busy
soil the worm passes through her gut
and the beetle swims in like a lake.

As I kneel to put the seeds in
careful as stitching, I am in love.
You are the bed we all sleep on.
You are the food we eat, the food
we ate, the food we will become.
We are walking trees rooted in you.

You can live thousands of years
undressing in the spring your black
body, your red body, your brown body
penetrated by the rain. Here
is the goddess unveiled,
the earth opening her strong thighs.

Yet you grow exhausted with bearing
too much, too soon, too often, just

as a woman wears through like an old rug.
We have contempt for what we spring
from. Dirt, we say, you're dirt
as if we were not all your children.

We have lost the simplest gratitude.
We lack the knowledge we showed ten
thousand years past, that you live
a goddess but mortal, that what we take
must be returned; that the poison we drop
in you will stunt our children's growth.

Tending a plot of your flesh binds
me as nothing ever could, to the seasons,
to the will of the plants, clamorous
in their green tenderness. What
calls louder than the cry of a field
of corn ready, or trees of ripe peaches?

I worship on my knees, laying
the seeds in you, that worship rooted
in need, in hunger, in kinship,
flesh of the planet with my own flesh,
a ritual of compost, a litany of manure.
My garden's a chapel, but a meadow

gone wild in grass and flower
is a cathedral. How you seethe
with little quick ones, vole, field
mouse, shrew and mole in their thousands,

124

rabbit and woodchuck. In you rest
the jewels of the genes wrapped in seed.

Power warps because it involves joy
in domination; also because it means
forgetting how we too starve, break
like a corn stalk in the wind, how we
die like the spinach of drought,
how what slays the vole slays us.

Because you can die of overwork, because
you can die of the fire that melts
rock, because you can die of the poison
that kills the beetle and the slug,
we must come again to worship you
on our knees, the common living dirt.

Ashes, ashes, all fall down

1.

We walk on the earth and feed of it;
we breathe in the air or we choke;
we drink water or die, but you:
you cannot enter us. No pain
is like your touch.

Once we lived wholly without you,
plucking fruit, digging roots, shaking
down nuts, scavenging like bears.
Our cousin mammals ignore or flee
your angry lion's roar.

Emblem of all we have seized upon
in nature, energy made property,
as what we use uses us; what
we depend on enslaves us; what
we live by kills us.

We stretch out our hands to the fire
place watching the colors shift
until the mind gives up buried images
like the secret blue in the log
the flame unlocks.

2.

Burning, burning, that fall I galloped,
the cries of torn children ringing
in my skull. Even cats mating in my Brooklyn

alley invoked images of thatched villages
scorched by bombing.

Burning, burning, I turned and roared
simple, loud as a trumpet blown, sonorous,
brassy, commanded and commanding. In that
heat everything dried from the inside,
baked to ashes.

Burning, burning we flared into sparks
where we touched. My back blistered.
My blood raced in a fire storm
to ignite mountains and valleys, a river
aflame in flood.

Burning, burning, I huddled over the cauldron
of my jealousy bubbling like hot lead.
Under my hilly day a fire in a coal mine
was smouldering, consuming invisibly
the solid earth.

3.

Passion simplifies like surgery.
We burn, and what we burn are the books,
the couch, the rug, the bed, the houseplants,
the friends who can't clear out
fast enough.

Yet a passionless life: all the virtues
gilded like saints in their niches

and nothing to move them. The architecture
of airports, laundromats. Cafeteria food
for the tepid will.

On one hand hopping along, a well appointed
portly toad licking up bugs, patrolling
the garden. On the other, flying
through the night like a skunked dog,
howling and drooling.

Burning, burning, we can't live
in the fire. Nor can we in ice.
Long ago we wandered from our homeland
tropics following game to these harsh
but fertile shores.

4.

On solstices, our ancestors leapt
through fire, to bring the sun around.
Surely some were not nimble enough
and a trailing scarf or skirt turned
burning shroud.

Without risk maybe the sun won't return.
Without risk gradually the temperature
drops, slowly, slowly. One day you notice
the roses have all died. The next year
no corn ripens.

128

Then even the wheat rots where it stands.
Glaciers slide down the mountains
choking the valleys. The birds are gone.
On the north side of the heart, the snow
never melts.

When I stare into fire, I see figures
dancing. People of our merry potlatch,
ghosts, demons or simply the memory
of times I have danced in ecstasy all night,
my hair on fire.

5.

Even breathing is a little burning.
The banked fire of the cells eats
oxygen like the arsonist's blaze.
All the minute furnaces stoked inside
warm our skin.

Life is a burning, and what we burn
is all the others we eat and drink.
We burn the carrot, we burn the cow,
we burn the calf, we burn the peach,
we burn the wine.

Life is a burning, and what we burn
is ourselves. Observe the back begin
to curl, to bow like a paper match

consumed, and the dark hair powdering
to grey ashes.

You are all we cannot live with
or without. You warm and you spoil,
you heat and you kill. Like us
whatever you touch, you seize for your use
and use up.

The pool that swims in us

1.

HELP STOP WETNESS cried the Arrid ads
that year. I used to leave you
and as the bus lurched westward on 14th
Street, from the slack of my pleased flesh
and the salty damp of my thighs
I would take comfort.

Wet is what flows and seeps and comes again:
that ocean we carry inside,
a tidal pool cherished from our spawning grounds
bottled to nourish us among alien rocks.
The sea is our ultimate, intimate ancestor.
Even trees cup sap that rises and falls.

Wet and sloppy the mutual joy
of stirring our bodies together
warm as breast milk.
We are wet jokes and wet dreams.
A scalpel slits us open like a busted
bag of groceries, and out we ooze.

Noses drip. Armpits sweat. Eyes weep.
We are born from a small salt pond
yet immersed in our own element we drown.
We have no natural habitat, we have

no home. We build shelters of trees
and stones and clay to keep us warm

from the wind and the water, and little
houses of wool and feather, to venture out.
We have been making a home badly for millennia.
The great contrary project
is to dry up the world by fire and turn
survivors into machines for making money.

2.

Our wise cousins, a million years past,
went home again. Dolphins have no houses,
no coins, no tools or tolls, no warehouses,
no armies, classes or taxes.
Dolphins in the sea help one another.
People among rock and cement
fear each other worse than the cyclone.

The standard way of making do up here
is to turn your neighbors into cattle,
hire guards to herd them, milk and breed them,
slaughter them. We incorporate
ten thousand years of bad habits,

habits of people training to be cattle,
habits of those who use others to fatten on.

3.

How can we feel part of one another?
How can we count the children of the trout
and the coyote and the humpback whale
as our relatives, when we cannot
believe somebody who makes half what
we do has as many feelings, that when small
black-haired people bleed, it's blood.

How can we feel part of one another?
Politicians say We, meaning I and my
flunkeys, my board of directors, we the five
percent of the people who own your bones.
They've insulted us in Katmandu we snarl
and wait for the missiles to avenge
our collective honor by random murder.

We must feel on our nerves the great pattern,
how the same water drifts in clouds across
our sky, blows on the rain in gauzy drifts,
gushes down storm drains. Swells the cabbage,

lengthens the grass blade the cow chews.
The same water rises from the well, runs
through us and falls to rush through sewers.

We are of one tide ebbing and flowing.
We are one circular pool. Ideas spread
in ripples. Diseases float their oil slicks.
The same waves cast us forward and free
or suck us drowning into vast cycles of boom
and bust. The same wars seize us, poison
our water and cast us up to die on strange beaches.

Acid rain from stacks in Akron, stuff
that coats the lungs of a choking rubber
worker, kills the pond in Wellfleet.
One river is gliding, spurting,
soaking through every living cell. The clam
that drinks the tide and the high-rise
dweller turning the faucet share that fluid.

We carry in the wet cuneiform of proteins
the long history of working to be human.
In this time we will fail into ashes,
fail into twisted metal and dry bones,
or break through into a sea of shared abundance

134

where man must join woman and dolphin and whale
in salty joy, in flowing trust.

We must feel our floating on the whole world river,
all people breathing the same thin skin of air,
all people growing our food in the same worn
dirt, all drinking water from the same
vast cup of clay. We must be healed at last
to our soft bodies and our hard planet
to make fruitful conscious history in common.

In 1968 I wrote a poem "In praise of salt and water," in-
cluded in *Hard Loving*. Ever since it has bothered me,
because it starts out right and then goes off into rhetoric,
seduced by postscarcity ideas I didn't truly believe even
when I wrote it. I decided to start over, and that was the
germ of this sequence, The Elementary Odes, growing
from that decision taken when I was putting together my
selected poems, *Circles on the Water*.

Stone, paper, knife

1.

It's a children's game: stone,
paper, knife. Paper covers stone,
knife cuts paper, stone breaks knife.

You lurch, guessing. You plot intentions
but you learn each one's strength and weakness
are light and shadows thrown by one source.

2.

I like plain pokers with luck
subordinate, bowing its golden
curly head, not games where
every red odd card is wild.

Grace shines in precisely doing
what the structure makes difficult.
When the team cheats, victory
is boring as Sunday real estate.

Games are the lighter rituals,
rules gravel paths pleasure follows.
Art is game only if you play at it,
a mirror that reflects from the inside out.

We like knowing what is to happen
with small surprises. But sometimes

we must endure or create gross shocks
that stretch us till we grow or break.

3.

The baby wants the same bottle
at the same time. The cat complains
when the easy chair is moved
from the fire. The dog brings back
the stick twenty times, wagging hard.

Stubbing my toe on habit,
a grave in the tall grass,
a stone hidden by weeds,
a metallic place in the mind,
a callus on the nerves.

Lush weeds overwhelm
our frail beginnings,
flowers set out in peat pots
watered once, abandoned
to choke in an overrun bed.

How easily we turn off the fingertips
like lightbulbs to save energy,
pull in from the nerve endings
capped like gleaming teeth,
then starve out impulse.

We make resolutions, bending
ourselves into daring new shapes,

137

thin strips of pliant wood.
When we loosen our grip,
we spring back as we were.

In repetition, a sense of identity
lulls, gathered into a tight ball
like socks in a drawer, mingled, woolly.
I am the one who puts honey in her morning
coffee, who won't eat anchovies, ham.

Me, remember me, don't sit in my
favorite chair, don't drink from my mug,
earth colored stoneware drawn
with serious cats. This typewriter
is just the right kind, and these pens.

Repetition numbs. How many men
I have lain with who would only
fit bodies together at one angle
and who required exactly muttered
obscene formulae, precise caresses

until every woman they embraced
was the same dolly of their will
and all coupling mechanical, safe
proceeding by strict taboos whose fabric
no wild emotion could pierce.

We cannot listen to every sound,
open as a baby, as a microphone,
to the furnace clanking on, the year's

last hornet butting on the pane,
the bare branch of locust rubbing,

the drier flutter of oak leaves,
the walls sighing, the pump coming on,
the dull thump of my heart working.
Focus is precise here and vague beyond,
willful narrowing of a field of vision.

We pay attention, spending now
and saving then. What should we
give over to habit like an old slipper
flung to the dog to chew, and what
should we save and strip?

4.

The wheel turns from solstice to solstice
when I light my candles and fires,
old rituals that quicken me toward death.

I keep birthdays for a week, I demand
presents shamelessly, rents
from all my properties of love.

I met my dear on Passover, so each seder
marks exit and entry, liberation
and a chosen bond. The meal I cook

gives me grandmother's face. That dance

of hands in the kitchen conjures dead
women who peek through me like a door.

I observe the full moon and the dark,
the cross quarters of the witches,
the pagan and the Jewish holidays

and our own three anniversaries:
when we met, when we first made
our love and when we made commitment.

Thanksgiving at dawn we begin to worship
with savory steam and sweet smoke. Feasts,
holy days give our passing dignity

as we shuffle round the circle dance
through seasons revolving stately as planets
from strong light slowly into the cold.

5.

Where do you want to return to, where
was it cozy, the hearth-fire-rose
that bloomed just for you on the mauve twilight?
What vast lap do you long to cuddle in
and suck what drug-spiked tit?
You can buy oblivion this year in fashion
shadows of dream, ivory and silver.

Is it power you recall entering fiery
in your chest like a shot of whiskey?
Was it love tolled you, a church
bell bonging every quarter hour,
played with rich reverberating changes
drowning out all thought and question
in that hammering peel of orchestrated want?

Or remembering when the children
were small, needs howled for you
every minute and broke the skin that formed
on the warm milk of your sleep,
how the sunflower faces followed you,
how the hands tugged at you hot
as open mouths, empty as midnight airports.

We can be addicted to the stone
of submission, of security, addicted
to the paper of mobility, blowing
lighter than dust and thin as water.
We can be addicted to the cleaver
of our will and go hacking through.
Security, power, freedom contradict.

How can we open our hands and let go
the old dangerous toys we clutch
hard, the mama dolls, the cowboy
six-shooters, the Monopoly sets,
the ray guns and rockets? How can we

with only stone and paper and knife
build with imagination a better game?

6.

Where out of our wavering half tainted
desires stained by the blood of mirrors,
drugged shuffling with apathy like Thorazine,
can we birth the hard clear image of hope?
For the ice shadows lengthen and the glaciers
begin their slow creeping dominion
over the heart, stilling its fervors.

For the wicked prance to public fanfares.
For the mean flourish the thunders
of righteous and religious rhetoric
like stolen purple banners, as if they
loved the earth and its children,
calling those who do not hate as well
as they hate, the fallen and low.

When evil tears the sun into bombs
that can burn the earth to its granite bones
and melt the limbs of children unborn;
when evil leaches subtle poison into the bright
waters, into the warm milk in the udder,
so women find strange lumps in their breasts,
so boys wither as their blood thins,

so men still handsome as bronze chrysanthemums
in October sunlight stoop as a wandering
blight travels from organ to organ;
when little girls are sold on the streets
like newspapers and women torn open and left
to bleed and the elderly freeze in hovels,
then who shall bear hope back into the world?

We give our government money to buy engines
of murder, torture abroad and want at home
while those who mined coal cough black blood,
while those who spun cloth die of brown lung,
while children sit hungry in crowded barren
schools sucking their fingers. Can hope
be born from us sulking in corners?

Who shall bear hope, who else but us?
After us is the long wind blowing
off the ash pit of blasted genes, or after,
the remarrying of the earth and the water.
We must begin with the stone of mass
resistance, and pile stone on stone on stone,
begin cranking out whirlwinds of paper,

the word that embodies before any body
can rise to dance on the wind, and the sword
of action that cuts through. We must shine
with hope, stained glass windows that shape
light into icons, glow like lanterns

borne before a procession. Who can bear hope
back into the world but us, you, my other

flesh, all of us who have seen the face
of hope at least once in vision, in dream,
in marching, who sang hope into rising
like a conjured snake, who found its flower
above timberline by a melting glacier.
Hope sleeps in our bones like a bear
waiting for spring to rise and walk.

A note about the author

Marge Piercy is the author of eight books of poetry:
*Breaking Camp, Hard Loving, 4-Telling, To Be of Use,
Living in the Open, The Twelve-Spoked Wheel Flashing,
The Moon Is Always Female,* and *Circles on the Water.*
She has also published seven novels: *Going Down Fast,
Dance the Eagle to Sleep, Small Changes, Woman on the
Edge of Time, The High Cost of Living, Vida,* and
Braided Lives. The University of Michigan's Arbor Press
published a volume of her essays, reviews, and interviews
as part of the Poets on Poetry Series entitled *Parti-
Colored Blocks for a Quilt.* She has also coauthored a play
with Ira Wood, *The Last White Class.* She lives in
Wellfleet, Massachusetts, with Ira Wood.

A note on the type

This book was set on the Linotype in Century Expanded, designed in 1894 by Linn Boyd Benton (1844–1932). Benton cut Century Expanded in response to Theodore De Vinne's request for an attractive, easy-to-read typeface to fit the narrow columns of his *Century Magazine*. Early in the nineteen hundreds Morris Fuller Benton updated and improved Century in several versions for his father's American Type Founders Company. Century remains the only American typeface cut before 1910 still widely in use today.

Composed by Maryland Linotype Composition Company, Baltimore, Maryland. Printed and bound by The Maple Press, York, Pennsylvania. Typography and binding design by Virginia Tan.

DATE			